STEPHEN BIRTSAS

The Modern Consultant

Mastering Mindset, Method and Meaning in the AI First Era

Contents

Prologue

Why This Book and Why Now

Consulting isn't what it used to be, and that's exactly the point.

We are in the midst of a seismic shift. Not the kind that creeps in unnoticed, but one that shakes the foundation of how companies operate, how decisions get made, and how value **is** created. If you're a consultant or aspire to be one, you're standing at the fault line between two eras. One foot planted in the world of frameworks, client whiteboards, and stakeholder workshops. The other in a world run by algorithms, digital twins, and autonomous systems making decisions faster than we can process them.

This book was born out of that tension.

In my work helping companies transform through digital innovation, I've seen firsthand what works and what doesn't. I've watched seasoned consultants struggle to connect strategy with execution in a world that's evolving faster than their slide decks. I've also seen brilliant new minds enter the field with curiosity, only to get lost in jargon and legacy methodologies that feel more academic than actionable.

So I wrote this book to serve as a bridge.

It's a collection of practical tools, mental models, and real-world stories designed for consultants who want to be better, not just at advising, but at adapting. It draws from decades of tried-and-true strategy frameworks, but reimagines them through a modern lens. It's for those who know the industry is changing and are ready to change with it.

This isn't a textbook. It's a field manual for the future of consulting.

Whether you're just getting started or leading your own practice, this book will challenge you to think differently about what it means to deliver value. It will arm you with approaches to thrive in the age of AI without losing the human core that makes great consultants invaluable.

Because no matter how smart the machines get, transformation still requires people who can ask the right questions, connect the dots, and lead others through uncertainty.

Let's begin.

1

What It Means to Be a Consultant Today

"If you still think consulting is about showing up with a polished slide deck and a black suit, you're already obsolete."

Welcome to the new era of consulting, one where authority isn't earned through tenure, knowledge is commoditized by AI, and clients have less time, more pressure, and higher expectations than ever before.

This isn't the consulting world I entered two decades ago, and that's exactly why you should be excited. Consulting today isn't dying, it's metamorphosing. The rules are changing, and if you're smart, adaptable, and relentlessly focused on impact, there has never been a better time to become a consultant. But if you're holding on to old playbooks, you're toast.

This chapter is your orientation and it starts by challenging what you think you know. Consulting is no longer about being the smartest person in the room. You've probably been told that consulting is about having the answers. It's not. Not anymore.

In a world where large language models like ChatGPT can generate a decent strategy in 30 seconds and every client has a McKinsey slide deck on file from 2014, being "smart" is table stakes. What clients really need is someone who can make sense of the noise, who can translate insight into action, and who can help them drive results when the stakes are high and the pressure is crushing.

That's what consulting is today: clarity, confidence, and forward motion.

Your Role Is to Create Movement, Not Just Recommendations

Too many consultants still operate with a "recommend and run" mindset. Here's the problem: no one cares how good your recommendations are if nothing changes.

Today, your role is not just to analyze or advise, it's to catalyze, to diagnose and drive. To architect solutions and ensure they're executed. You're not there to be admired. You're there to make things happen.

In a modern engagement, clients don't just want answers; they want acceleration. They're looking for translators, builders, change agents, and coaches. They want you in the arena with them. Not on the sidelines, narrating the play.

From Analyst to Architect to Operator

In today's market, the most valuable consultants are multi-dimensional. You can't just be a good researcher or strategist. You need to move fluidly between three modes:

1. Analyst – Break down the problem, separate signal from noise and frame the challenge.
2. Architect – Design the solution, think in systems, align people, process, data and technology.
3. Operator – Drive execution, build momentum, adapt on the fly, and deliver outcomes.

Clients don't want specialists who can only do one. They want hybrids who can span the full arc of transformation.

Consulting Isn't Glamorous. It's Gritty.

Let me be brutally honest: consulting isn't about traveling the world in business class, collecting hotel points, and taking selfies in front of whiteboards. At least not if you're doing it right.

Real consulting is hard. You're managing ambiguity, navigating politics, battling inertia, and often working with incomplete information, tight deadlines, and conflicting agendas. But if you're wired for impact, there's nothing more rewarding than helping a client solve something they didn't think was solvable.

If you're addicted to growth for your client and yourself, this work will stretch you in ways no classroom ever could.

Consulting in the AI-First World

Here's the punchline: the machines aren't coming for our jobs. They're coming for our excuses.

AI is automating the easy stuff. That's good. Because it frees you up to do the work that actually matters, the work that requires human judgment, emotional intelligence, and strategic thinking. You'll use AI to speed up discovery, enrich insights, and prototype faster. But don't make the mistake of thinking clients will pay you for what AI can do better, faster, or cheaper. They'll pay you for what only a great consultant can do: make the complex actionable, align people around change, and turn potential into performance.

The Consultant's Contract (Unwritten, But Real)

Every time you walk into a client's office, physically or virtually, you're entering into a silent agreement. It goes something like this:

"I'm trusting you to tell me the truth, help me make sense of what's happening, and move me toward a better future. You don't have to be perfect, but you do have to care."

This is the code we live by.

It means owning outcomes, not just deliverables. It means making the client better, even after you're gone. It means putting ego aside and putting your client and their success first.

Your Mission from Day One

If you're just starting your consulting career, here's your mission:

- Learn fast. Listen deeply.
- Be obsessed with impact, results, and the value delivered.
- Always remember that a solution that nobody uses has no value.
- Never lose your trust, character, and moral compass.
- Ask "why" until it makes sense, and then ask "why not" until it gets better.
- Use tools, frameworks, and AI, but don't hide behind them.
- Make the team better. Make the client smarter. Make the outcome real.

Final Thought: You Weren't Hired to Blend In

You weren't hired to blend in. You were hired to make a difference.

So don't play small. Don't wait to be told what to do. Don't be afraid to speak up, respectfully challenge, or offer a new way forward. The world doesn't need more consultants. It needs better ones. Consultants who understand the moment we're in and rise to meet it.

Welcome to the arena. Let's get to work.

2

The Consulting Mindset

"If you want to succeed in consulting, stop trying to be the expert in the room. Start becoming the most useful person in the room."

You can learn frameworks. You can practice analysis. You can fake confidence. But mindset? That's different.

Mindset is what shows up when things get ambiguous, political, or chaotic. It's what separates the consultant who's just collecting experience from the one who's delivering results and building trust that lasts careers. This chapter is about that mindset. The one you need to thrive, not just survive, in the modern consulting world.

Spoiler: It's not about being smarter. It's about how you think, show up, and respond when the pressure is on.

Curiosity Beats Certainty

The worst consultants are know-it-alls. The best ones are question-askers.

The moment you think you have all the answers is the moment you stop being useful. The modern consultant is relentlessly curious. You don't assume. You investigate. You listen like a detective and dig like an archaeologist.

You ask:

- "Why is this really happening?"
- "What are we not seeing?"
- "Who benefits from the status quo?"
- "What would we do if we weren't afraid?"

In a world full of noise, curiosity is your superpower. It cuts through surface-level thinking and gets you to the heart of the issue, where the real value lies.

Extreme Ownership (Without Control)

Here's the paradox: You're responsible for results... but you don't control the resources, the people, or the politics. Welcome to consulting.

That's why great consultants develop extreme ownership. You

take accountability for the outcome, not just the work. You act like it's your name on the business, your budget on the line, your people at stake. That doesn't mean doing everything yourself. It means showing up with solutions, anticipating blockers, following through, and never saying, "That's not my job."

If the project fails, you don't point fingers. You ask: "What could I have done differently to prevent that?". This mindset builds trust faster than any credential ever will.

Confidence Without Arrogance

Yes, your clients want smart. But they also want safe.

They want someone who can walk into a room, hold the space, synthesize complexity, and say, "Here's what I see. Here's what I recommend. Here's how we start."

Confidence matters, but only when it's paired with humility.

Consultants who posture, name-drop, or pretend to have all the answers? They lose the room fast. The best consultants speak simply, ask honestly, and listen with intent. They know when to take the lead and when to let others shine.

Pattern Recognition Over Templates

In consulting, you'll be tempted to reuse the same playbook. Same framework, different client. Same deliverable, different logo.

Don't fall for it!

Modern consulting is about pattern recognition, not template regurgitation. You need to learn how to see the structure beneath the noise. Spot what's really going on, even if it's hiding behind incomplete data, corporate politics, and resistance to change. Patterns are what allow you to bring speed without sacrificing relevance. But you've got to do the work first. You've got to see before you solve.

Adaptability Is Your Insurance Policy

Let's be real: no project goes exactly as planned. The strategy shifts. The sponsor leaves. The timeline shifts. The data is wrong. The client doesn't adopt.

And that's okay if you're ready for it.

Consultants who cling to the plan will break. Consultants who flex, evolve, and adjust will thrive. Adaptability is what keeps your value intact when the terrain changes. It's how you stay relevant when the scope creeps or the market shifts mid-engagement.

Ask yourself:

- Can I reframe the problem mid-flight?
- Can I reset expectations with confidence?
- Can I bring new ideas when the old ones fall flat?

If yes, you're already miles ahead of most.

Gravitas Without Ego

Gravitas isn't about being loud. It's about being intentional.

It's the quiet strength that makes people lean in. The ability to pause before speaking. To simplify the complex. To speak with precision and purpose. Gravitas comes from preparation, self-awareness, and clarity, not from being the center of attention. In a world filled with noise, the consultant who can bring calm, presence, precision, and a plan is rare. And extremely valuable.

Client Empathy: Understand the Pressure They're Under

Consulting isn't just about solving the business problem. It's about understanding the human behind the business. Your client might be under immense pressure. Career on the line.

Budget cut. Boss breathing down their neck.

You have to see that, feel that, and design your engagement with empathy.

That means:

- Making them look good in front of their peers.
- Helping them communicate your ideas like they were their ideas.
- Understanding their motivations and their fears.

People don't remember how great your analysis was. They remember how you made them feel when everything was on fire.

The Mindset Summary: How You Show Up

So here's your cheat code for the modern consulting mindset:

- Curious, not cocky.
- Accountable, not controlling.
- Confident, not arrogant.
- Calm, not passive.
- Empathetic, not enabling.
- Agile, not chaotic.
- Simple, not simplistic.

That's the mindset that earns trust, delivers results, and builds a lasting career.

Field Challenge: Practice the Mindset

This week, try this:

1. Ask five "Why?" questions in your next client meeting.
2. Identify one assumption you're making and challenge it.
3. Write down one moment you owned the outcome (even if it wasn't your fault).
4. Catch yourself in a moment of ego and replace it with curiosity.

These habits will shape your mindset more than any training or certification ever could.

Final Word: You Are the Product

Remember: in consulting, you are the product. Your mindset is your interface.

So, before you master the frameworks or memorize the jargon, build the mindset. That's what keeps you valuable, regardless of how fast the tools change. This is the foundation. Every great consultant I've worked with, every rainmaker, every transformation leader, every trusted advisor, they all had this mindset burned into their DNA.

Make it your edge.

3

Mastering the Consulting Process

"If you can't explain how you get from the problem to impact, you're not consulting, you're guessing."

Every elite consultant I've worked with has something in common. It's not where they went to school. It's not their industry background. It's not even their technical skill.

It's that they know how to think through a problem, systematically, flexibly, and fast.

That's what this chapter is about: the consulting process that turns ambiguity into clarity, and clarity into results. This is the scaffolding beneath every high-impact engagement I've ever led. It doesn't guarantee brilliance, but it guarantees traction.

If you want to stop faking it and start owning the room, you need to master this.

The Modern Consulting Life Cycle

Let's start with the big picture. Here's the real consulting life cycle, used by top firms and transformation leaders, adapted for the AI-first era:

1. Discovery
2. Problem Framing
3. Hypothesis Development
4. Data Collection and Analysis
5. Insight Generation
6. Solution Design
7. Stakeholder Alignment
8. Execution and Change Management
9. Value Realization

You don't need to treat this as a rigid waterfall. This is not a checklist. It's a rhythm. A set of gears. You will loop back. You will adjust. But if you skip a gear, the whole thing breaks.

Let's break it down.

1. Discovery: Don't Solve the Wrong Problem

Before the kickoff meeting, before the SOW, before the first slide, you need to ask: What are we actually solving for?

Most engagements are born from symptoms:

- "Our margins are shrinking."
- "Our customers are churning."
- "Our tech stack is a mess."

But symptoms aren't problems. Your job is to discover what's beneath the surface.

Ask:

- What does success look like to the client?
- What decisions are being blocked?
- Who's pushing for this and why now?

This stage is about understanding the why, not just the what. If you don't get this right, everything else is a waste of time and money.

2. Problem Framing: Clarity Is a Competitive Advantage

Consulting is a clarity business.

You win by defining the problem better than the client can. That's what earns you the right to solve it. We use issue trees, MECE structures, and reframing techniques to carve chaos into categories. But more important than the tools is the discipline: you don't move forward until the problem is crystal clear and mutually agreed upon.

A well-framed problem:

- Is outcome-oriented ("How can we reduce lead time by 30%?")
- Has boundaries
- Ties directly to value

Without it, you're swinging in the dark.

3. Hypothesis Development: Don't Analyze Blind

Let me be contrarian here: consulting is not about being objective. It's about being hypothesis-driven. You don't wait for the data to tell you something; you tell the data what you expect, then test it. This hypothesis-driven approach was popularized by firms like McKinsey & Company and is a cornerstone of structured consulting thinking.

Why? Because hypotheses:

- Focus your analysis
- Accelerate your insight
- Force you to make assumptions explicit

Come in with "smart guesses," pressure-test them fast, and iterate. This is how top consultants move with speed and precision.

4. Data Collection and Analysis: Dig Deep, Move Fast

Data is no longer a bottleneck; it's an avalanche.

Your job is to:

- Prioritize what data actually matters
- Pressure-test its reliability
- Extract signal, not noise

Use AI and automation tools here; they should be your sidekicks. But never outsource thinking to the tool.

5. Insight Generation: Make It Click

Great analysis is useless unless it leads to insight. Insight isn't a fact; it's a truth that drives action. Insights are not a perfectly designed dashboard. Insights uncover the truth and help to illuminate the path forward.

Ask yourself:

- So what?
- Why does this matter now?
- What would change because of this?

Your job is to connect the dots and make the client see something they couldn't before. This is achieved by following the first five steps:

1. Discover the Situation
2. Frame the Problem
3. Hypothesize
4. Analyze and Test Your Hypothesis With Data
5. Develop and Deliver Insights

Insights don't just appear, it takes work. You must go through the process to understand the situation, frame the problem, develop a working hypothesis, analyze and test the hypothesis with data, and uncover the insights that will allow you to meaningfully help your client.

How to Move From Data to Insights:

	DATA	INFORMATION	FINDINGS	INSIGHT
What It Tells You	Raw facts and figures without context or interpretation.	Data that has been organized, processed, or structure so it has meaning.	Results or outcomes discovered through analysis of information.	A clear explanation of the underlying cause and what action to take.
Example	"500 units sold"	"Sales = 500 units in Q2"	"Sales fell 20% in Q2"	"Sales fell because price increases alienated loyal customers"
Purpose	Input for analysis	Understand what happened	Show patterns or changes	Enable informed decisions & actions

But even after all this work, insights alone don't influence people. You must compellingly present your insights and influence your client to take action. Remember, your role is to create movement, not just recommendations.

This is why storytelling is so important and necessary to communicate your insight clearly to drive action, change, and results.

As an example, you could present the above insight to describe how a 20% sales drop in Q2 was linked to recent price hikes. I often do this through storytelling and use of simple analogies that bring out emotion. In this example, it helps the client feel the same emotion that their customers are feeling and understand from the customer's perspective why they are leaving.

If I were presenting this to my client, I might start by asking a question and telling a personal story. For example, I might lead by saying, "Do you remember a time when one of your favorite companies raised their prices so high, it made you question the value and ask yourself, is it still worth it? I remember when my kids' barber raised his price almost 40 % and even though my kids really liked the barber, we knew we could find someone else at a better value, and we did." I would then proceed to explain to my client that they're doing the same thing to their loyal customer base, and it's eroding their sales. I would then proceed to tell them, "If only the barber reached out to me, explained why he was raising his prices, asked me for my thoughts, or raised them 20% rather than 40%, I would likely still be a customer." I'd then go on to present and support our findings relative to the company's data, with clear visuals and analyses, and I'd show they are in the exact same position as our barber. Loyal customers are disengaging and impacting their business. I would then present multiple data-driven scenarios for adjusting pricing and customer outreach campaigns to regain those customers to reverse the trend.

If you don't deliver at least one insight that makes the room go silent, you're not done yet.

6. Solution Design: Build with the Client, Not for Them

Clients don't buy brilliance. They buy into a belief that you will help them be successful, and you can't do that in a vacuum. Don't disappear into a room and reemerge with a masterpiece. Co-create. Whiteboard. Prototype. Test and iterate.

A modern solution isn't a report, it's a playbook, a system, a model, a set of tools and behaviors that people can use and adapt.

Always design solutions to deliver the value that the client is expecting. This means you must design solutions for adoption, not applause. For transformation and change, not status quo. Design with the end user in mind. If the client doesn't use it, I can guarantee, it will never deliver the expected value.

7. Stakeholder Alignment: Influence Is the Work

If the right people aren't on board, the right solution doesn't matter.

You need to:

- Map stakeholders (sponsors, influencers, resistors)
- Tailor your message to their priorities
- Pre-wire decisions before the meeting
- Listen, adapt, and keep people informed

This is political. Emotional. Messy. But it's also the most human part of consulting, and often where trust is forged.

8. Execution and Change Management: Don't Just Recommend—
Drive It

You can hand over a strategy. Or you can drive a transformation.

Modern consultants do the latter.

That means:

- Building workplans, milestones, and action owners
- Training and enabling teams
- Adjusting on the fly when the wheels come off
- Staying close to the ground and elevating wins

Change is hard. But when you walk the path with your client, it
becomes possible.

9. Value Realization: Impact Is the Only Score That Matters

This is where great consultants separate themselves from the
herd.

You don't stop when the work stream ends. You stay focused
on:

- Are we seeing the results?
- Are behaviors changing?
- Are KPIs moving?
- Is the organization sustaining this?

This is where you quantify the ROI, tell the value story, and lock in your legacy. You don't wait to track value, you start from day one, and you course-correct if the path isn't delivering. You relentlessly pursue outcomes, not just milestones.

The Process in Motion

Let's be clear: you won't always follow this linearly. Real life isn't clean.

Sometimes you'll frame a problem and discover you've missed the real issue. Sometimes a stakeholder throws a wrench in your execution plan. Sometimes your "great idea" flops on the ground floor. That's okay. The process isn't about perfection; it's about traction. When you know this rhythm, you can flex, pivot, and rebuild on the fly. And when you bring your client along for the ride, you build credibility that lasts careers.

Final Word: The Process Is Your Anchor

In a world of shifting priorities, AI acceleration, and organizational chaos, the process is your anchor. It gives you a way to navigate uncertainty with structure. It gives your client confidence that there's a method to the madness, and it gives you the ability to deliver value repeatedly, no matter what's thrown at you.

Master this process, and you won't just be doing consulting. You'll be leading it.

4

Frameworks That Work

"Frameworks are tools, not trophies. If you're just showing off models instead of solving problems, you're missing the point."

Let's get something straight: frameworks are not magic.

They're scaffolding. They're lenses. They're shortcuts to clarity. But on their own, they don't solve anything. In the wrong hands, they confuse. In the right hands, they unlock insight at speed.

In this chapter, we'll talk about how to use frameworks like a modern consultant, not like a textbook robot. We'll unpack the essential ones, when to use them, how to adapt them, and just as important, when to ignore them.

Spoiler: clients don't care how many models you know. They

care how fast you can help them see clearly, decide confidently, and move forward with impact.

The Purpose of a Framework

At its core, a framework does three things:

1. Simplifies complexity – It takes a big, messy problem and gives it structure.
2. Creates common language – It aligns stakeholders on what we're actually talking about.
3. Accelerates insight – It helps you spot patterns, gaps, and levers for action.

That's it. A framework is a thinking tool, not a final product. Don't fall into the trap of using them to look smart. Use them to make others smarter.

Frameworks Aren't Plug-and-Play

One of the most common mistakes junior consultants make is grabbing a slide from the "Great Deck Archive" and forcing it into the situation.

Wrong move.

Every client is different. Every problem is contextual. That's why modern consultants customize, combine, and reframe frameworks to fit the moment. You're not a delivery robot. You're a solution designer; real design starts with listening, not copying and pasting.

The Essential Frameworks (and When to Use Them)

Below are the go-to frameworks I've used across Fortune 500 transformations. Not to impress, but to progress.

1. MECE (Mutually Exclusive, Collectively Exhaustive)

What It Is

MECE is a problem-structuring principle that ensures your thinking is both complete and non-overlapping. It helps consultants break down complex issues into clean, logical buckets that cover the full problem space without duplication. MECE is foundational for structured thinking and clear communication.

Origin

Coined by Barbara Minto in *The Pyramid Principle*[1] (2009), MECE became popular within McKinsey & Company and remains a core tool in consulting toolkits. It underpins much of how consultants build issue trees, structure decks, and synthesize data.

When to Use It

- Structuring problems, solutions, or hypotheses
- Designing frameworks or taxonomies
- Organizing presentation content
- Conducting brainstorming or root cause analysis

How It Works

- Break down a topic into categories where:
- Mutually Exclusive = no overlap between categories
- Collectively Exhaustive = nothing left out

For example, if analyzing customer types, segmenting by demographics and behaviors separately may avoid overlap and ensure full coverage.

To apply MECE:

- Define the problem or subject clearly.
- Break it into first-level categories that are MECE.
- Continue decomposing where needed.
- Test for overlaps or gaps and revise.

Benefits

- Improves clarity and logic in communication
- Enables more efficient analysis and synthesis

- Creates clean slides and easier stakeholder alignment
- Reduces risk of double-counting or missed issues

An Illustrative Example

Here's a simple example. Consider the challenge of categorizing all fruits in a grocery store. To apply the MECE principle, we could break the category "fruits" into "citrus fruits," "berries," and "stone fruits." Each fruit belongs to one and only one group (mutually exclusive), and together, these categories cover every type of fruit in the store (collectively exhaustive). For example, lemons fit under citrus, strawberries under berries, and peaches under stone fruits, with no overlaps or items left out. This clear, logical structure prevents confusion, ensures comprehensive coverage, and makes analysis or communication far more effective.

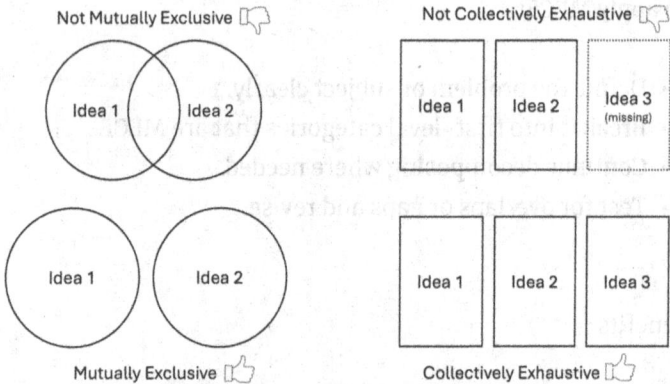

Not Mutually Exclusive

Idea 1 Idea 2

Mutually Exclusive

Idea 1 Idea 2

Not Collectively Exhaustive

Idea 1 | Idea 2 | Idea 3 (missing)

Collectively Exhaustive

Idea 1 | Idea 2 | Idea 3

2. Issue Trees / Logic Trees

What It Is

An issue tree (or logic tree) is a visual breakdown of a complex problem into component parts. It helps consultants explore potential causes or solutions in a structured, cascading format.

Origin

Issue trees evolved from systems thinking and root cause analysis practices. Popularized within strategy consulting firms like McKinsey, they are a core part of structured problem solving.

When to Use It

- Diagnosing a performance or process issue
- Breaking down business questions into manageable parts
- Framing hypotheses and data collection
- Structuring collaborative problem-solving sessions

How It Works

Start with a central question or problem at the top. Break it down into mutually exclusive, collectively exhaustive branches (often using MECE). Continue decomposing each branch until it leads to testable hypotheses or actionable drivers.

Two common types:

1. Diagnostic Trees (why is X happening?)
2. Solution Trees (how can we achieve Y?)

To apply:

- Define the problem as a central question.
- Break into first-level drivers using MECE logic.
- Decompose until you reach specific, testable root causes or levers.
- Use the tree to guide your analysis.

Benefits

- Breaks big problems into actionable parts
- Makes logic and assumptions explicit
- Aligns team thinking and next steps
- Serves as a visual roadmap for investigation

An Illustrative Example

A manufacturer experiencing frequent leaking of a facial mois-ture cosmetic package used an issue tree to diagnose possible root causes. The tree decomposed the root cause of the leaks across material, design, manufacturing, and/or distribution/

handling problems into a mutually exclusive and collectively exhaustive (MECE) list of possible root causes, allowing the team to quickly analyze and identify the root cause of the leak to address the problem.

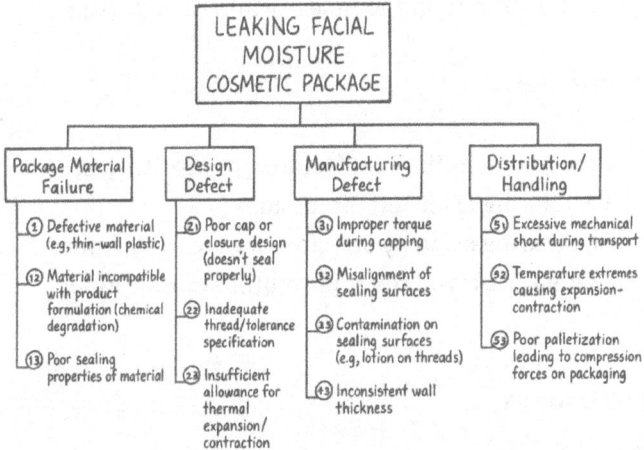

3. 2x2 Prioritization Grid

What It Is

A 2x2 Prioritization Grid is a decision-making tool that visually maps options across two key dimensions, enabling clearer prioritization and trade-off discussions. It helps executives get unstuck by seeing choices in context.

Origin

Used extensively by BCG, McKinsey, and product strategy teams, the 2x2 matrix is inspired by visual decision theory models. It's a go-to for simplifying complexity into a single page.

When to Use It

- Prioritizing initiatives, features, or investments
- Facilitating trade-off discussions
- Structuring strategy off-sites or exec workshops
- Comparing risks, costs, or returns across options

How It Works

Draw a two-axis matrix (X and Y) using the two most critical dimensions for decision-making (e.g., Impact vs. Effort, Cost vs. Risk). Plot options into the four quadrants.

Common Axes:

- Impact vs. Effort
- Urgency vs. Importance
- Risk vs. Return
- Cost vs. Complexity

To apply:

- Select decision criteria (axes).
- Facilitate discussion to rate or score initiatives.
- Plot items visually.
- Use bubble size or color to add a third variable (e.g., value, cost).

Benefits

- Drives clarity and alignment fast
- Supports executive decision-making in real time
- Helps make implicit trade-offs explicit
- Works well in workshops and white boarding

An Illustrative Example

During a strategic planning session, an industrial equipment manufacturer used a 2x2 grid to prioritize digital initiatives. By plotting projects across "Cost" and "Complexity," they quickly aligned leadership around fast wins and long-term investments, reducing debate and accelerating funding decisions.

OPPORTUNITY PRIORITIZATION 2 x 2

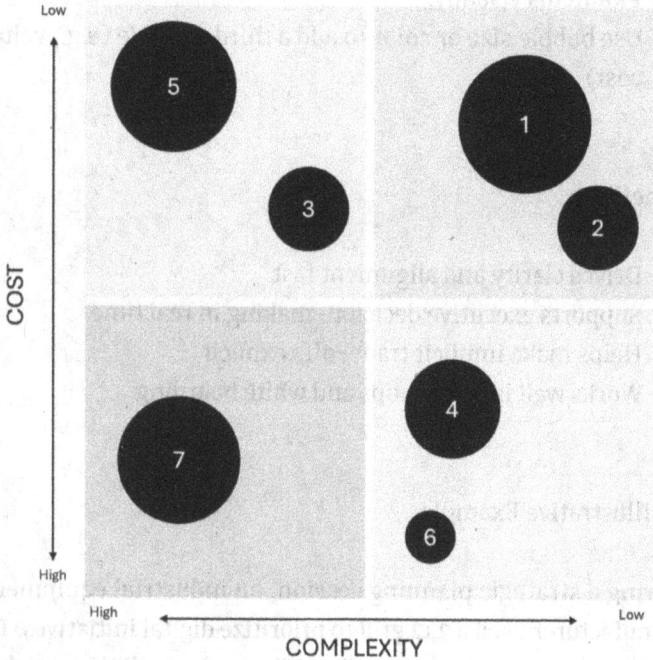

Pro tips:

- Don't present it as the answer; use it to guide the conversation.
- You can use bubble size as a third dimension, such as value, as shown in the example above

4. GE McKinsey Matrix (9-Box)

What It Is

The GE McKinsey Matrix, often called the "9-Box", is a strategic portfolio analysis tool used to prioritize investments across multiple business units, products, or initiatives. It helps leaders decide where to grow, hold, or divest by evaluating each area based on two dimensions: industry attractiveness and internal business strength.

Unlike simpler models like the 2x2 matrix, the 9-Box provides a more nuanced and multi-factor analysis, offering greater depth in portfolio decisions.

Origin

Developed jointly by McKinsey & Company and General Electric in the 1970s, the matrix was created to help GE manage its complex and diversified portfolio of businesses. The model evolved from early strategic planning frameworks, combining financial rigor with a visual, executive-friendly format.

When to Use It

- Evaluating a portfolio of business units, products, or markets
- Prioritizing investments or resource allocation
- Supporting corporate strategy, divestiture, or M&A decisions

- Assessing growth opportunities or transformation focus areas

How It Works

The matrix has 9 cells formed by crossing two axes:

- Y-axis: Industry Attractiveness (e.g., market size, growth rate, profitability, competitive intensity)
- X-axis: Business Unit Strength (e.g., market share, capabilities, brand strength, cost position)

Each unit is plotted into one of the 9 cells:

- Top right (Grow) – Attractive industry, strong position
- Middle (Selectively Invest or Hold) – Moderate attractiveness or strength
- Bottom left (Divest or Harvest) – Weak position in a weak market

To apply:

- Define the portfolio of businesses or initiatives.
- Score each against pre-defined criteria for both dimensions.
- Plot them in the matrix.
- Use the position to guide strategic choices: grow, hold, or exit.
- Layer in bubble size to represent size of revenue, investment,

or value.

Benefits

- Enables fact-based, visual portfolio decisions
- Encourages focus on where to win, not just where to compete
- Builds alignment across strategy, finance, and operations
- Supports M&A, transformation, or investment planning
- More flexible and nuanced than the 2x2 or BCG matrix

Real-World Example

During their annual business planning sessions, a leading professional services firm employed the GE McKinsey Matrix to strategically evaluate their suite of service offerings. Each service line was evaluated for attractiveness in each industry that they served and their existing capabilities to deliver those services in the regions where they compete.

The matrix revealed clear patterns: services in fast-growing sectors were placed in the "Invest & Grow" quadrant, prompting increased investment and resource allocation; stable but saturated offerings were categorized as "Hold," indicating the need to maintain performance but limit new investments; meanwhile, legacy services with declining relevance were evaluated and some were identified for "Exit," with a phased plan developed for redeploying resources.

This visual, fact-based approach helped leadership prioritize where to double down, where to sustain, and where to step back, ultimately aligning teams from sales, professional services, capability teams, operations, finance, and marketing shaping a focused, actionable portfolio plan for the year ahead.

GE McKinsey Matrix "9-Box"

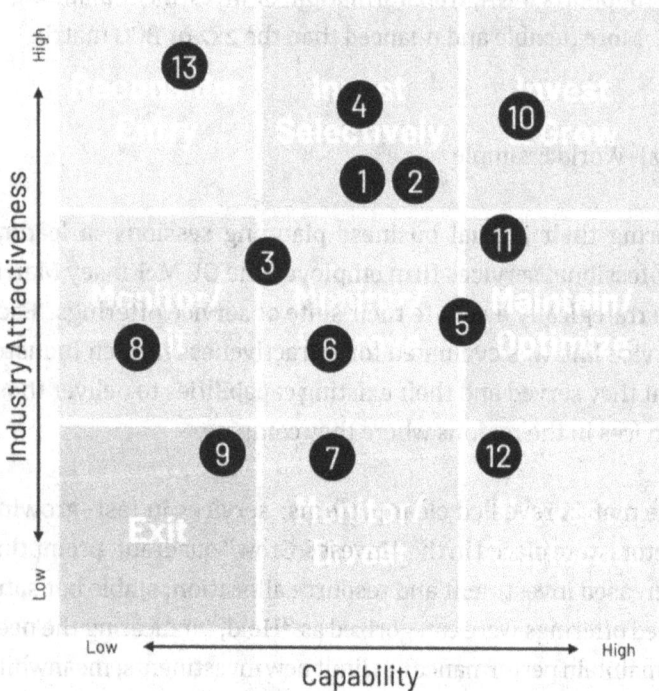

5. Value Chain Analysis

What It Is

Value Chain Analysis is a framework that maps all the activities a business performs to deliver a product or service, from raw inputs to customer delivery. It helps identify where value is created, where it leaks, and where transformation can generate impact.

Origin

Introduced by Michael Porter in *Competitive Advantage* (1985)[2], the framework categorizes business activities into primary and support activities. It remains foundational in strategy and operations consulting.

When to Use It

- Diagnosing operational inefficiencies
- Designing cost-reduction or value-creation programs
- Supporting transformation and digitization initiatives
- Analyzing product or process profitability

How It Works

The value chain is divided into:

1. Primary Activities – Inbound logistics, operations, out-

bound logistics, marketing & sales, and service.
2. Support Activities – Firm infrastructure, HR, technology development, and procurement.

To apply:

- Map the business's activities into the value chain categories.
- Layer in metrics like cost, time, margins, or digital maturity.
- Identify value creation areas and leakage points.
- Propose improvement or transformation levers.

Benefits

- Offers a full-system view of operations
- Identifies cost drivers and profit pools
- Helps prioritize digital or process improvement investments
- Supports cross-functional alignment on transformation goals

An Illustrative Example

A global snack food company used Value Chain Analysis to optimize its potato chip manufacturing operation. By analyzing their capabilities and performance across the value chain from inbound receiving to outbound shipping. They identified automation gaps in peeling, slicing, and frying, limited data, and data quality to improve their automation capabilities

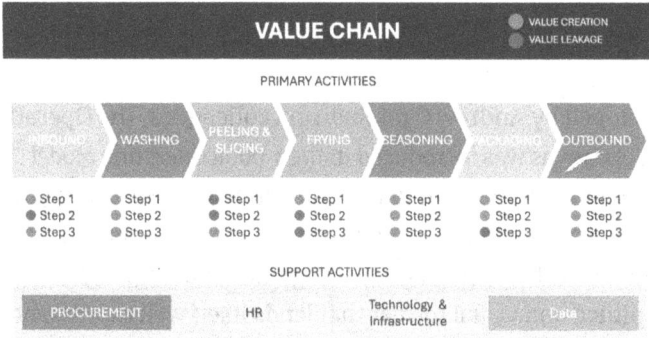

6. Operating Model Canvas

What It Is

The Operating Model Canvas is a strategic framework that helps organizations design and align their operating model to effectively deliver on their business strategy. It breaks down an organization's way of working into six interdependent components, making it easier to visualize, assess, and transform how value is created and delivered.

Unlike high-level strategy tools, the Operating Model Canvas bridges the gap between strategy and execution by focusing on the operational choices and organizational structure required to bring a strategy to life.

Origin

Developed by Andrew Campbell and colleagues, the Operating Model Canvas was introduced in their book *Operating Model Canvas: Aligning Operations and Organization with Strategy*[3] *(2017)*. It builds on the legacy of the Galbraith Star Model (Galbraith, 2002) and other organization design methodologies, but with a simplified and visual format that lends itself well to workshops, executive discussions, and transformation programs.

When to Use It

- You need to translate strategic intent into tangible operational plans.
- You're designing a new business unit, function, or enterprise model.
- You're supporting a digital transformation, M&A integration, or cost optimization effort.
- The client organization lacks alignment across structure, systems, and ways of working.
- You want to create a shared view across cross-functional teams of how the business should operate.

How It Works

The Operating Model Canvas is structured around six core elements, commonly remembered by the acronym POLISM:

1. Processes – The critical value-creating activities that must be performed effectively
2. Organization – The people, roles, reporting lines, and accountability structures
3. Location – Where the work is performed and how location impacts operations (e.g., distributed teams, regional hubs, centers of excellence)
4. Information – The systems, data, and knowledge required to support decision-making and execution
5. Suppliers – The external partners, vendors, and ecosystems that support delivery
6. Management System – The governance, performance management, leadership, and cultural enablers that ensure the model functions cohesively

To use the framework:

- Start with the business strategy and define the required outcomes.
- Map out the current state of each POLISM element.
- Identify gaps or misalignments relative to strategic goals.
- Co-design the target state operating model across all elements.
- Prioritize transformation initiatives needed to close the gap.

Benefits

- Visual clarity – Helps non-technical stakeholders understand complex operations

- Strategic alignment – Ensures operating decisions are grounded in the organization's strategic goals
- Cross-functional utility – Useful across business, HR, IT, and transformation teams
- Modular and adaptable – Works for entire organizations or individual functions, geographies, or business units
- Supports transformation – Ideal for defining a target operating model (TOM) and guiding change programs

Real-World Example

A global consumer goods company launched a direct-to-consumer (DTC) channel for the first time. Consultants used the Operating Model Canvas to map out the new requirements across all six POLISM components. This helped the client visualize what needed to change e.g., new fulfillment processes, customer data systems, digital marketing capabilities, and a flatter organization structure and prioritize investments accordingly.

OPERATING MODEL CANVAS		
PROCESS	**ORGANIZATION**	**LOCATION**
● New fulfillment process for DTC orders	◉ Flatter structure with Digital Marketing team	● New fulfillment center distribution
INFORMATION	**SUPPLIERS**	**MANAGEMENT SYSTEMS**
● New consumer customer data systems and insights	● E-commerce platform provider	◉ Consumer digital marketing capabilities

● New
◉ Change

General Guidance On the Use of Frameworks

Know the "Why" Before the "What"

Never drop a framework into a deck because it "looks smart."

Ask:
   What problem is this solving?
   What clarity does this unlock?

Adapt Language to the Client

Ditch the jargon. If the framework uses terms that don't match how your client talks, translate them. Make it their own.

Visual is greater than Verbal

Great frameworks are visual because clients think in pictures. Draw, whiteboard, sketch—it'll make your insight stick.

Don't Force It

If the model doesn't fit the problem, don't use it. Build your own. Blank whiteboard > misapplied framework.

Framework Fails (and How to Avoid Them)

I've seen it too many times:

- Framework Overload: Throwing 5 models into a deck just to look "thorough."
- Consulting Bingo: Dropping terms like "Porter's Five Forces" in places where they don't belong.
- Client Confusion: Using frameworks to obscure insight, not reveal it.

Avoid these traps. Remember, clarity wins.

Story Time: When a Whiteboard Beat a 100-Slide Presentation

We were in a war room with a Fortune 100 COO. A competing firm had just pitched a transformation strategy with a 110-slide deck, full of models, matrices, and heat maps.

She looked at us and said, "Make it simple."

We walked to the whiteboard. Drew a 2x2. Labeled the axes: "Operational Risk" and "Strategic Value." Plotted the top 10 initiatives. Talked through trade-offs.

Ten minutes in, she said, "That's what I needed."

The framework didn't win the room. Clarity did.

Final Word: Think Before You Framework

Frameworks are the sharpest tools in your consulting toolbox if you use them with purpose. Don't use them to look clever, use them to make others confident. The best consultants don't worship frameworks; they wield them. Know them, adapt them, evolve them, and when needed, create your own.

Because the most powerful framework is the one that gets your client to say:

"Now I get it. Let's move."

5

Data-Driven, Outcome-Focused

"If your insights don't lead to action—and your actions don't lead to value—then you're not consulting. You're just commenting."

We live in a world where data is everywhere. It's on dashboards, buried in Enterprise Resource Planning (ERP) systems, floating in Product Lifecycle Management (PLM) systems, hiding in spreadsheets, and if we're being honest, trapped in the heads of employees who have been doing things the same way for 20 years. Yet, for all the buzz around "data-driven decision-making," most organizations still struggle to use data to drive results.

That's where you come in.

As a modern consultant, your job isn't to present data. It's to transform it into insight, into action, into measurable value. This chapter is about how to do that with precision and purpose.

Start with Outcomes, Not Output

Let's begin with a consulting sin that's all too common: delivering a polished analysis... with no impact.

I don't care how impressive your graphs look. If they don't help the client solve a real business problem or make a better decision, they're noise.

Start here: "What outcome are we trying to drive?"

Be specific. Not "optimize operations" or "improve customer experience." That's vague fluff. Aim for:

- "Reduce cost-to-serve by 12%"
- "Improve delivery lead time from 10 days to 5 days"
- "Increase cross-sell conversion rate by 3 points"

When you start with the outcome, your analysis becomes a weapon, not a wall.

Define Success Early and Explicitly

Want to really build credibility with clients? Be the person who walks in and says, "Let's define success now, not at the end."

Here's what that sounds like:

- "What KPIs matter most to you?"
- "How will we know if this project created real value?"
- "If we delivered everything you asked for but nothing changed, would you still call it a success?"

You're not just managing a work plan; you're managing expectations, alignment, and accountability. And here's the kicker: once you've defined success, you're allowed to say no to things that don't move the needle. That's freedom.

Measure What Matters

Not all metrics are created equal. Here's the cheat code:

Metric Type — Purpose

- Leading Indicators: Predict future performance (e.g., number of demos booked)
- Lagging Indicators: Confirm performance (e.g., revenue growth)
- Operational KPIs: Track process health (e.g., cycle time,

scrap rate)
- Behavioral Metrics: Gauge adoption and behavior change

Great consultants know which metrics to track, when to track them, and how to present them. Don't overwhelm with numbers, focus on meaning.

Make the Value Visible

Your job isn't just to deliver insights. It's to prove value.

That means:

- Building a simple, client-facing value tracker from day one
- Capturing baseline performance data before the intervention
- Quantifying the potential value of recommendations (even if directional)
- Connecting operational wins to financial outcomes (e.g., "This saves 5 hours per shift → That's $300K in labor efficiency")

You want your client to see the scoreboard and know you helped move it.

Storytelling with Data: The Real Skill

Raw data doesn't move people. Stories do.

Modern consultants are data translators. You turn messy facts into sharp narratives.

Here's the structure:

1. What are we seeing? (Observation)
2. Why does it matter? (Implication)
3. What should we do? (Recommendation)
4. What will it achieve? (Value)

Don't just drop a graph in the deck. Walk the client through it. Highlight the "aha." Help them feel the opportunity or the risk.

Data should build confidence and urgency, not confusion.

Use AI, Don't Get Used by It

AI is changing how we approach analysis. Fast!

But here's the truth: AI isn't replacing consultants. It's replacing slow, average, reactive consultants.

You should be using AI to:

- Analyze large datasets in seconds
- Surface anomalies, trends, and patterns
- Generate initial hypotheses
- Automate dashboards and visualizations
- Enrich your findings with external benchmarks and sentiment

But you are still responsible for the thinking. For context. For judgment. For connecting the data to the human decisions that matter.

AI is your co-pilot, not your conscience.

Common Pitfalls (And How to Avoid Them)

Mistake 1: Data for Data's Sake
  "Look at all this analysis!"
  Cool. What do I do with it?

Fix: Every slide, every metric, every chart must pass the "So what?" test.

Mistake 2: Ignoring the Human Factor
  "The data proves the system works."
  Sure, but are the people using the system?

Fix: Combine quantitative and qualitative. Interview. Observe. Validate. Insights live at the intersection of people and numbers.

Mistake 3: Hiding Behind Ambiguity
"We don't have perfect data."
Welcome to consulting.

Fix: Directional > Precise. Estimate, triangulate, make assumptions transparent, and move forward.

Your Value Narrative

At the end of every project, you should be able to answer these questions in one crisp sentence each:

1. What changed?
2. What did we improve?
3. How much did it matter?
4. How do we know?

If you can't answer that... did you actually deliver value?

Field Challenge: Make It Measurable

In your next client engagement:

- Ask for 3 baseline metrics in the first week
- Build a value tracker into your weekly cadence
- Use AI to prototype your first analysis in 1 day
- Present 1 insight using narrative plus visualization
- Tie your recommendation to a dollar amount (even direc-

tional)

Repeat this every time. Make value part of your identity.

Final Word: Outcome Over Optics

The consulting industry has too many polished slide decks and too few clear results.

Don't be that kind of consultant.

Be the one who asks the hard questions. Who ties every idea to a measurable outcome. Who makes the value visible, early, often, and loudly.

Data is your flashlight. Insight is your map. Outcomes are your north star.

Stay focused on the scoreboard, and make it move.

6

AI and the New Consulting Toolkit

*"You don't need to be replaced by AI to become irrelevant.
You just have to keep working like it doesn't exist."*

Consulting has always been about speed, clarity, and impact. Now, the bar's even higher. Clients expect you to move faster, see further, and deliver value yesterday. Meanwhile, the competition isn't other firms, it's tools that work 24/7, cost nothing to run, and learn faster than you can read.

That's not the end of consulting. That's the start of something better for those who adapt.

This chapter isn't about AI as a buzzword. It's about AI as your unfair advantage if you're smart enough to use it and bold enough to evolve your game.

Consulting Is Changing — Fast

- The old version of consulting: "Smart people with frameworks and whiteboards."
- The new version: "Smart people with AI copilots, insight velocity, and real-time value creation."

Today's consultant doesn't just think, they augment. You're not faster than a machine, but you can be smarter when you work with one.

AI Is the New Analyst (If You Know How to Use It)

Let's be clear: AI won't run your client meetings, decode corporate politics, or build trust with a skeptical CFO.

But AI can:

- Draft your first 80%
- Supercharge your research
- Analyze a mountain of data in minutes
- Summarize 10 stakeholder interviews before your coffee gets cold
- Translate strategy into code, process maps, or user stories

The modern consultant's edge is no longer about who works harder. It's about who leverages better tools and who applies them with better judgment.

The New Toolkit: What to Use and How to Use It

Large Language Models (LLMs)

Use for:

- Hypothesis generation
- First-draft proposals
- Client communication drafts
- Idea generation and reframing

Pro Tip: Use prompt chaining, build on each output with targeted follow-ups. You'll go from average to elite output fast.

AI-Enhanced Analytics

Use for:

- Natural language querying of data
- Pattern recognition
- Auto-building dashboards and insight summaries

Pro Tip: Teach your AI tools how you think, feed them KPI definitions and preferred data views. Make them your partner, not a stranger.

Voice + Meeting AI

Use for:

- Capturing meeting minutes without taking notes
- Creating stakeholder maps from transcript analysis
- Extracting action items and sentiment signals

Pro Tip: Don't just rely on the transcript. Run it through a LLM prompt like: "Summarize key objections and power dynamics."

Document Intelligence

Use for:

- Scanning document data sources
- Building knowledge maps
- Identifying previously solved problems or reusable assets

Pro Tip: Build a reusable internal AI agent trained on your past proposals, reports, and playbooks. Let your legacy work compound.

Your Role Is Shifting, That's a Good Thing

AI can replicate knowledge. But it can't replicate:

- Your presence in the boardroom

- Your ability to challenge a VP with the perfect question
- Your sensitivity to when a stakeholder is bluffing
- Your instinct to reframe a doomed strategy mid-project

You're no longer the calculator. You're the conductor. You're orchestrating people, tools, tech, politics, and pressure to create real transformation. AI handles the repetitive. You deliver the remarkable.

How to Ethically and Strategically Use AI in Consulting

The fastest way to ruin trust? Misuse AI.

Here's the modern consultant's AI code:

Own the Output. If AI generates a deck, recommendation, or memo, it's still your name on the slide. Validate, refine, and contextualize.

Don't Feed It Client Data Blindly

Use enterprise tools with compliance guardrails. Always follow your company's AI and security policies and ask before using AI: "Would I email this data to a third party?" Do not underestimate the ethical, legal, and compliance aspects of AI.

You are accountable and responsible for how you use AI and the data that you expose to AI.

Be Transparent When It Matters: You don't need to explain every prompt. But if a core insight was AI-assisted, don't fake it. Clients respect augmentation, not deception.

Your AI-Powered Workflow: A Day in the Life

Start of day:

- Ask your AI: "Summarize all unread client emails and Teams messages."
- Get briefed. Faster.

Mid-morning strategy call:

- Use AI meeting notes to extract decisions and emotional tone shifts.
- Flag risk areas for client lead follow-up.

Afternoon client analysis:

- Use Business Intelligence and Reporting Copilots: "Compare product line profitability over 6 quarters."
- Refine your hypothesis. Share visuals.

Evening:

- Prompt your LLM: "Draft a recap email that highlights momentum and value created."
- Review it, send it. Sleep well.

Field Challenge: Elevate Your Consulting with AI This Week

Try these:

- Use a LLM to draft your next stakeholder interview guide.
- Ask it to summarize a prior project's lessons learned.
- Prompt it to compare two strategies and stress-test both sides.
- Use AI to recap your internal team meeting.
- Automate the first draft of your next presentation outline.

Track how much time and mental load you save.

Final Word: You + AI = The Modern Consultant

AI isn't a threat. It's a filter. It's filtering out the lazy, the slow, the ones who can't evolve. But for the bold? For the curious? For the ones who see AI as an accelerant, not a competitor?

It's fuel.

Don't wait! Start building your AI-augmented consulting muscle now. The next era of consulting isn't about who's smartest. It's about who's fastest to insight, closest to value, and most trusted to lead.

7

Stakeholder Mastery

"The biggest variable in every project isn't the solution—it's the people who have to believe in it."

Let's tell the truth: consulting isn't really about frameworks or deliverables or clever recommendations. It's about stake-holders, the messy, brilliant, fearful, ambitious human beings who ultimately decide whether your work lives or dies. You can have the best insight, backed by the best data, wrapped in the cleanest deck, and still fail. Why? Because you didn't master the human dynamics.

This chapter is about the art and science of stakeholder mastery. How to read the room, earn influence without authority, navigate politics, and build coalitions of believers. If you get this right, everything else in consulting gets easier.

Consulting Is an Influence Business

Here's the hard truth: Clients don't always pick the best idea. They pick the idea they believe in, trust, and feel ownership of. That means your job isn't just to deliver analysis. It's to help people see, believe, decide, and act.

And you have to do that with:

- No formal authority
- Limited time
- Often incomplete information
- And sometimes active resistance

That's why stakeholder mastery isn't a nice-to-have; it's a core consulting skill.

Map the Stakeholder Landscape (Not All Stakeholders Are Equal)

Don't treat the client organization as a flat list of names. It's an ecosystem, and you need to map it.

Start by identifying:

- Decision Makers: Who has the power to say yes or no?
- Influencers: Who shapes opinions behind the scenes?
- Blockers: Who benefits from the status quo?

- Champions: Who is emotionally invested in success?
- Fence-sitters: Who hasn't decided yet—and why?

A simple stakeholder map beats any fancy slide. It clarifies:

- Who you need to win over
- What matters to them
- How much risk they perceive
- What their informal networks look like

Build Relationships Before You Need Them

The best consultants don't wait until a big decision is looming to connect with stakeholders.

They build trust early:

- One-on-one conversations to understand personal motivations
- Casual check-ins to build rapport
- Showing genuine curiosity about their world, pressures, and goals

Why? Because when crunch time comes, decisions happen based on relationships, not reports.

Tailor Your Communication for Each Stakeholder

There is no "one size fits all" communication strategy.

You have to meet people where they are:

- The CFO? Lead with numbers and ROI.
- The operations lead?   Show practicality and impact on execution.
- The frontline manager? Acknowledge effort and implications for their teams.
- The skeptical VP? Anticipate objections and address them proactively.

This isn't manipulation. It's empathy plus strategy.

The Art of "Pre-Wiring" Decisions

Want to ace your next steering committee? Don't treat it as the place where decisions get made.

Instead:

1. Identify key decision-makers before the meeting.
2. Meet with them individually.
3. Walk them through your recommendation in advance.
4. Listen to objections, adjust if needed, and build alignment.
5. Use the meeting to confirm consensus, not create it on the

spot.

This is called "pre-wiring," and it's how elite consultants get things done.

Read the Room in Real-Time

Meetings are where stakeholder mastery shows up in real-time.

Pay attention to:

- Who's speaking, and who's not.
- Body language, eye contact, and tone shifts.
- Side comments and subtle objections.
- Decision fatigue, impatience, or skepticism.

Adapt your approach on the fly:

- Slow down if the energy feels confused.
- Summarize and synthesize if you sense overload.
- Bring in quiet stakeholders explicitly if they hold influence.

Consultants who can read a room win trust faster than any slide deck ever will.

Manage Resistance with Empathy

Resistance isn't always hostility. Sometimes it's fear, fatigue, or just competing priorities.

Your job is to:

- Understand what's behind the resistance (Is it fear of failure? Loss of status? Misalignment on priorities?)
- Validate legitimate concerns
- Engage constructively not defensively
- Offer a path forward that feels safe and pragmatic

The consultant who can de-risk adoption for stakeholders becomes indispensable.

Influence Without Authority = Power Skill

Here's the paradox of consulting:

- You don't have formal power.
- You don't have control over resources.
- You often don't even work for the client's company.

Yet you're expected to lead.

That's why influence without authority is the defining consulting skill.

It's about building credibility fast:

- Showing up prepared, thoughtful, and articulate.
- Creating psychological safety so stakeholders can speak openly.
- Being trusted as an advisor, not seen as a hired gun.

Field Challenge: Master the Stakeholder Map

In your next engagement:

1. Identify 5 key stakeholders early (don't wait for formal org charts).
2. Set up one-on-ones with them within the first two weeks.
3. Map their motivations, fears, and influence networks.
4. Pre-wire any major recommendation before presenting it in a large group.
5. Track who's leaning in, who's leaning out and why.

This will give you leverage most consultants miss.

Final Word: The Human Side Is the Hard Side

AI can write slides. It can draft analyses. It can summarize meetings. But it can't read a room, build trust, or navigate power dynamics. That's your job. In a fast-moving, AI-accelerated world, your mastery of stakeholders will be the single most irreplaceable consulting skill you develop.

Remember:

- Consulting is a people business.
- Influence is the work.
- Trust is the currency.

Become indispensable by becoming an expert in the human side. That's how you stop being a vendor and start being a trusted advisor.

8

Running Great Consulting Projects

*"Great consultants don't just deliver work—they deliver
outcomes. Running a project well is the ultimate test of
whether you can turn smart ideas into measurable,
lasting impact."*

The Reality of Consulting Projects Today

Every project begins in uncertainty. The client may think they
know what they want, but often they aren't entirely sure—
and that's okay. Your job isn't just to follow the brief. Your
job is to lead a journey from ambiguity to clarity, from inertia
to momentum, from strategy to sustained results. You'll be
asked to juggle evolving client needs, competing priorities,
limited resources, and complex politics, all while creating the

perception that the project is under perfect control.

The secret? It's not about perfection, it's about mastering the disciplines, mindsets, and rhythms that drive momentum and value, even in imperfect conditions.

The Consultant's Project Leadership Playbook

At the heart of every successful consulting project is a core operating model that balances structure and flexibility:

1. Define and frame the problem well.
2. Design a plan with clear milestones, but build adaptability into it.
3. Maintain a relentless focus on delivering value (not just deliverables).
4. Manage stakeholders proactively to reduce surprises and resistance.
5. Create a steady cadence of progress, accountability, and communication.

Sounds simple. But doing this well separates average consultants from trusted advisors.

Relentless Focus on Value

Here's the trap most consultants fall into:

They manage the project as if "completing the work" is the goal. But in today's consulting world, completing a project on time and budget isn't enough. You need to show that you've delivered business outcomes that matter.

How to execute with a value-first mindset:

Define success before you start

Explicitly align with your client on measurable outcomes—not just activities. Example: "We're not just implementing software. We're reducing order cycle time by 20%."

Establish metrics and baselines on day one

How will we measure improvement? What's the current state? Without clear starting points, you can't credibly claim impact later.

Track value through every phase

Every workstream, milestone, and recommendation should directly tie back to measurable outcomes.

Course-correct if the value is slipping

Be bold: If what you're doing isn't producing the intended results, change the approach. Clients respect consultants who protect outcomes more than plans.

Human-Centered Change: Value Only Happens When People Adopt

Here's the uncomfortable truth: "No matter how brilliant your solution, it will fail unless people adopt it." Sustained value realization depends entirely on behavior change.

The human-centered change principles:

- Involve stakeholders early and often.
- Co-creation creates ownership. People support what they help build.
- Assess readiness for change early.
- Don't wait until go-live to discover adoption risks. Interview teams, map concerns, measure sentiment, and address it head-on.

- Communicate with empathy, not just logic.
- Business cases don't change behavior. Stories, relevance, and clear "what's in it for me" narratives do.
- Celebrate early adopters and quick wins.
- Create momentum and social proof that the change is working.

Designing Momentum and Discipline

Momentum is essential. Even brilliant strategies will stall without energy and progress.

How modern consultants keep projects moving:

- Establish rituals:
- Daily stand-ups
- Weekly checkpoints
- Monthly steering committees

These aren't just meetings, they are mechanisms for clarity and focus.

Make progress visible:

- Simple dashboards
- Value trackers
- Visual roadmaps

When clients see progress, they feel momentum, and they stay engaged.

Remove ambiguity quickly. Consultants who clarify next steps, decisions, and risks before the client even asks earn trust fast.

Scope Discipline + Flexibility

Consulting projects are rarely static. Requirements shift. Stakeholders change. Priorities evolve. Elite consultants manage scope carefully, but they stay adaptable:

Clarify scope boundaries upfront

Use the statement of work as a living document, not a contract to weaponize, but a reference to align expectations.

Document scope changes as trade-offs

Example: "If we expand the analysis to include additional sites, we will need to shift the timeline or add resources."

Ensure the scope always serves the value case.

If a change doesn't add value? Push back constructively.

Execution at the Speed of Trust

Execution excellence comes down to trust:

- Trust in your process
- Trust between the consultant and the client
- Trust that everyone is aligned and rowing in the same direction

You build that trust by:

- Showing up prepared and consistent
- Anticipating and addressing client concerns before they escalate
- Communicating proactively, no surprises
- Sharing bad news fast, with a solution already in mind

Field Challenge: Become a Project Value Steward

In your next engagement:

RUNNING GREAT CONSULTING PROJECTS

- Set a clear "value narrative" on day one: What are we trying to achieve and why?
- Create a simple "Value Tracker" that aligns every milestone to a measurable business outcome.
- Assess change readiness in the first two weeks: Identify likely adoption barriers early.
- In every weekly update, communicate progress against value, not just tasks.
- Adapt your project plan any time value creation comes under threat; don't wait for formal change control to act.

Final Word: The Consultant as Project Leader

Great consulting projects don't happen by accident.

They're led by consultants who:

- Balance structure and agility
- Design momentum and clarity into every phase
- Focus relentlessly on value realization
- Understand that no project succeeds without people embracing change

At the end of the day, your project plan, frameworks, and KPIs are just tools. What matters is that you leave your client measurably better than you found them and that you ran a project that felt purposeful, well-led, and human. If you can do that? You won't just run great projects. You'll run great transformations.

9

Becoming a Trusted Advisor

"Trusted advisors don't just get hired—they get invited
into the conversations that matter most."

In today's consulting world, becoming a trusted advisor is the pinnacle of your professional evolution. It's what separates vendors from partners, and it's where the most interesting work and durable client relationships live. It's also where AI won't touch you. AI can draft reports and crunch numbers, but it can't earn trust.

In this chapter, we'll take inspiration from one of the most foundational works on this topic: *The Trusted Advisor*[4] by David H. Maister, Charles H. Green, and Robert M. Galford (2000). They didn't just define the concept; they gave us a practical, timeless formula for what trust is and how to build it. That formula, known as The Trust Equation, is the perfect framework for this chapter.

Why Trusted Advisor Status Is Your Endgame

Let's be clear: clients have endless choices for advice, data, and expertise. But they have far fewer people they truly trust.

Trusted advisors:

- Get called before the client even fully knows what they need
- Are invited into sensitive, high-stakes discussions
- Influence beyond their official remit
- Create long-term, mutually valuable relationships

In short: this is where consulting becomes not just lucrative but impactful, lasting, and fulfilling.

The Trust Equation: The Formula for Building Trust

Maister, Green, and Galford's The Trusted Advisor offers a deceptively simple yet profound formula for understanding how trust is built:

Trustworthiness = (Credibility + Reliability + Intimacy) / Self-Orientation

Let's break this down carefully.

Credibility

Credibility is about what clients believe you know.

It's demonstrated through:

- Your expertise
- The clarity of your analysis
- The logic of your recommendations
- The confidence with which you communicate

How to increase Credibility:

- Communicate clearly and simply. Complex language erodes credibility. Clear language boosts it.
- Demonstrate subject matter expertise without arrogance. Bring facts, data, and frameworks, but don't hide behind them.
- Be willing to say, "I don't know, but I'll find out." Honesty beats bluster every time.

Reliability

Reliability is about what clients believe you will do.

It's your consistency over time:

- Do you show up prepared?
- Do you follow through on what you promise?
- Can they count on you, week after week?

How to increase Reliability:

- Deliver small promises consistently, not just big ones.
- Create dependable rhythms (weekly updates, regular check-ins).
- Anticipate client needs so they never have to chase you for next steps.

Intimacy

Intimacy is about emotional safety.

It's what clients feel when they can share sensitive, even vulnerable information with you:

- Are you empathetic?
- Are you discreet?
- Do they feel they can be candid with you?

How to increase Intimacy:

- Build rapport beyond the transaction, and understand them as people.
- Be a safe sounding board when they're under pressure.

· Show genuine care about their success, not just your project.

Self-Orientation

This is the denominator in the Trust Equation and where many consultants fail. It measures whether clients sense that you are more focused on your own agenda than on their success. If your client perceives that your primary interest is:

· Winning the next engagement
· Impressing your boss
· Scoring points internally at your firm

...then trust collapses.

How to reduce Self-Orientation:

· Make every interaction about the client's needs, context, and challenges.
· Avoid self-promotion in meetings. The best Consultants let their work speak for itself.
· Ask more questions than you answer. Listen without an agenda.
· Help your client look good in front of their stakeholders.

How to Apply the Trust Equation Every Day

Here's the key insight from The Trusted Advisor:

Trust isn't just built in formal settings; it's built in hundreds of small moments. In every interaction, you can ask yourself:

- Am I being clear, direct, and credible?
- Am I reliable? Have I done what I said I would do?
- Am I demonstrating empathy and creating safety for this client?
- Is my focus on them, or am I focused on myself?

The Trust Equation gives you a diagnostic lens you can use in real time, every day.

How Trusted Advisors Think and Behave Differently

Trusted advisors:

- Spend more time listening than talking.
- Don't rush to prove they're smart.
- Seek to understand the client's definition of success, not impose their own.
- Anticipate the client's emotional landscape, not just their business needs.
- Are willing to challenge their client's assumptions with respect, tact, and courage.

In short: they think like an extension of the client's leadership team, not as an external service provider.

Field Challenge: Practice the Trust Equation This Week

In your next client engagement:

- Before each meeting, ask yourself: "Am I focused on them or me?"
- In your next presentation or conversation:
- Demonstrate expertise (Credibility)
- Deliver on small promises (Reliability)
- Engage with empathy (Intimacy)
- Keep ego out of the room (minimize Self-Orientation)
- At the end of each week, reflect: Did I build trust? Where did I erode it? Where can I improve?

Final Word: Trust is Your Currency—Guard It Relentlessly

The Trusted Advisor reminds us that trust is hard-earned and easily lost. In a fast-moving, AI-accelerated consulting landscape, where frameworks and expertise are increasingly commoditized, trust is your most valuable asset. Mastering the Trust Equation gives you a roadmap for earning, deepening, and sustaining that trust, not just during a project, but across your entire career. This is the work that transforms a consultant into a true advisor.

And once you achieve that? You won't just get projects, you'll get a seat at the table where real change happens.

Note: The Trust Equation and key insights referenced in this chapter and throughout this book are drawn from The Trusted Advisor by David H. Maister, Charles H. Green, and Robert M. Galford (2000). It is highly recommended reading for every consultant seeking to master the craft of trust-based advisory work.

10

Growing Relationships, Accounts, and Building a Sustainable Business

"If you think account growth is about cross-selling services or pushing for a bigger SOW, you're missing the point. It's about building trust so deep and value so clear that clients ask you back before they even know what they need."

Consulting is a relationship business. Always has been. Always will be. But what those relationships look like and how you nurture them has changed.

Today, growing a book of business isn't about playing golf, sending holiday gifts, or schmoozing your way onto a preferred vendor list. It's about being indispensable. About showing up as an extension of the client's leadership team. About knowing their business, industry, ecosystem, and pressures so well that you become their go-to call, not their optional vendor.

It requires work: real relationship building, clear account

planning, and a mindset of professional eminence that evolves with today's realities.

Relationships Before Revenue

Let's be brutally honest: clients know when they're being sold to, and they hate it.

Growing accounts today is about relevance and trust, not persuasion. Your mission: build a relationship map that goes beyond your day-to-day contacts. You need to know:

- Who's really making the decisions?
- Who influences them behind the scenes?
- Who controls the budgets?
- Who's quietly blocking progress?
- Who will champion you when no one's looking?

You can't wing this. Modern consultants build and maintain relationship maps that help them navigate complex organizations. They review them often, update them as people move, and use them to anticipate needs.

But here's the thing: relationship maps aren't just about names and org charts—they're about understanding motivations, fears, pressures, and ambitions. When you deeply understand what keeps a stakeholder up at night, you stop pitching and start helping.

Account Planning Is a Verb, Not a Deck

Traditional account plans? Static documents that sit on a shelf.

Modern account planning? A living process, a tool you actively use to drive momentum and deepen trust.

Here's what a modern account plan must do:

- Clarify the client's strategic priorities over the next 12–24 months (not just what they've hired you to do now).
- Map their internal politics and decision processes.
- Identify whitespace: unmet needs, latent problems, emerging risks.
- Establish concrete next steps for how you will grow the relationship without feeling transactional.

The best consultants treat account planning like they treat stakeholder management: dynamic, iterative, and human.

Professional Eminence—Redefined for the Modern Era

In the past, "building eminence" meant writing a whitepaper, speaking at an industry conference, or cultivating niche expertise over decades.

That playbook is gone.

Clients don't care if you're "well-regarded." They care if you're visible, relevant, and accessible right now.

Professional eminence today means:

Being seen as an authority by the people who matter to your clients, which increasingly means showing up in digital spaces like LinkedIn, podcasts, and industry forums.

Sharing insights that aren't generic trend reports, but hyper-relevant takes on what's happening in their business, industry, and ecosystem. Bringing fresh ideas before they ask for them.

But here's what hasn't changed: you can't fake expertise. You have to earn it. That means going deep in an industry, function, or capability so that when clients think of that space, they think of you first. In short: your professional reputation is now an active asset you cultivate, not a credential you collect.

Grow Accounts by Growing Trust

Here's the truth about sustainable book growth: it's not about selling more, it's about being more useful.

The modern consultant:

- Anticipates needs: They don't wait for an RFP; they're already talking about the problem the client doesn't know they have yet.

- Challenges assumptions: They're willing to gently but firmly tell the client when they're heading down the wrong path.
- Builds coalitions: They use their relationship map to engage decision-makers, influencers, and skeptics alike.
- Stays relevant: They keep learning and evolving so that every interaction adds value, even if no immediate project is attached.

Play the Long Game

A sustainable book of business is exactly that: sustainable. Not dependent on one hero project or one key relationship. Diversified, resilient, and driven by trust.

That means:

- Balance your portfolio: Don't get comfortable with one big account or a single industry. Diversify your relationships across clients, sectors, and geographies.
- Protect the relationships, even when there's no active project: Check in, share relevant insights, and offer help without a hidden agenda.
- Remember that every interaction compounds: You're always planting seeds. Sometimes they bloom in three months. Sometimes in three years.

The Consultant's Relationship Contract

Here's your unwritten contract when it comes to account growth:

"I will invest in relationships before I ask for revenue. I will focus on making my client successful in ways that go beyond the immediate scope of work. I will build trust so strong that my client calls me first, before they even know what they need."

This mindset is what separates the average from the exceptional.

Field Challenge: Build Your Relationship and Account Muscle

This week, try this:

- Identify one key client where you can build or refresh your relationship map. Document the stakeholders, their roles, their motivations, and their influence.
- Draft a living account plan for that client: What are their top 3 business priorities right now? Where can you add value next? What's the next conversation you should initiate?
- Post or share one public insight that demonstrates your relevance and expertise in a domain that matters to your client.
- Reach out to one contact before you need to; just to check in, share something useful, and nurture trust.

Final Word: Relationships Are the Work

At the end of the day, growing accounts isn't a separate activity from delivering great consulting; it's the natural byproduct of showing up as a trusted advisor who makes clients smarter, faster, and more successful.

In an AI-first world where frameworks, analysis, and even content are increasingly automated, relationships remain human and invaluable. The modern consultant understands this: your relationships are your real asset. Treat them with care. Build them with intention. And keep evolving how you show up, so your relevance and your book of business endures.

11

Life on the Inside — Consulting as a Career

"Consulting isn't just a job—it's a lifestyle. And if you don't take responsibility for how you live it, it will take control of you."

The Myths vs. The Reality of a Consulting Career

We've heard the myths:

- Consulting is all prestige, travel, fine dining, and fast-track promotions.
- Work hard enough and success naturally follows.

But here's the reality:

Consulting is a demanding, high-pressure profession where your success depends not only on your client impact but also on how well you manage your energy, health, relationships, and mindset. It's a marathon disguised as a series of sprints, and those who thrive long-term are those who figure out how to sustain themselves while delivering excellence.

The Valley of Despair: My Defining Lesson

Early in my consulting career, I learned this the hard way, a phase I now call "The Valley of Despair."

At that point in my life, I was working 70–80 hour weeks, flying cross-country every Monday morning, flying home exhausted every Thursday night, and trying to maintain a façade of balance in my personal life.

Outwardly, I was "successful." Inwardly, I was burned out, disconnected, and barely keeping up. At the deepest part of that valley, I came to a realization: I had a decision to make.

I could:

1. Decide that consulting was simply not the career for me and walk away.

or

2. Consciously take control of my career, my time, my health, my

relationships, and find a way to make this profession sustainable and fulfilling.

I chose the latter, and that decision changed everything. From that moment forward, I applied the following principles from this chapter:

- I built boundaries to protect my time and energy.
- I prioritized my relationships with intentionality.
- I treated my body and mind with the respect they deserved.
- I shifted from a passive "victim of the consulting lifestyle" to an active architect of my personal and professional life.

Throughout my career, I've been through multiple valley's but the first "Valley of Despair" was the hardest and also the most important. It taught me that consulting, my career, and my personal life would never be sustainable unless I took control.

And here's the truth I want you to take from this:

Throughout your life, you'll face many valleys, but that first time you decide who you are and define the principles that you will operate by going forward will change your life. Once you make the decision that your destiny is in your hands, your life and career will change.

Respect for Your Body, Mind, and Relationships

After that moment, everything I did flowed from this mindset shift:

I wasn't going to let consulting run my life. I was going to run my consulting life.

My Three Principles

1. Treat Your Body with Respect

- Exercise became non-negotiable. I scheduled workouts like client meetings and protected that time ruthlessly.
- Nutrition became fuel, not an afterthought. No more fast-food dinners at 9 PM every night.
- Sleep became sacred. I learned that good decision-making, patience, and focus are impossible when I was sleep-deprived.

2. Protect Your Mind and Mental Health

- I carved out time for reflection and focus, not letting every moment be filled with noise and tasks.
- I cultivated resilience practices that worked for me, whether it was reading, mindfulness, journaling, or simply walking without distraction.

3. Honor Your Relationships

- I stopped treating personal time as "what's left over after work."
- I blocked time for me, family, friends, and meaningful personal activities and kept those commitments as seriously as any client meeting.
- I communicated openly with those close to me about my rhythm and availability, so I could sustain their trust and support.

The Power of Boundaries: Time Management for Life and Work

A pivotal shift for me was redefining what time management meant. It's not just about being efficient, it's about being intentional:

- Prioritizing what truly matters, professionally and personally.
- Saying no or renegotiating deadlines when needed to protect quality and sustainability.
- Batch processing low-value tasks so they don't clutter prime thinking hours.

The Consulting Lifestyle Can Be Sustainable—But Only If You Own It

Here's what I realized looking back:

Before I consciously took control, I was letting the consulting lifestyle happen to me. Afterward, I was designing my consulting lifestyle around my values, health, and relationships. That shift didn't hurt my career; it accelerated it.

I became a better consultant:

- More focused
- More creative
- More patient
- More empathetic to clients who were themselves overwhelmed and burned out

And I became a better leader:

- Modeling balance and sustainability for the teams I mentored
- Teaching others how to stay sharp, resilient, and present over the long term

The Valleys Will Keep Coming—But You'll Handle Them Differently

Even after that first Valley of Despair, I hit many smaller valleys throughout my career:

- When clients were especially demanding
- When travel schedules got intense
- When personal life felt stretched thin

But having made that first conscious decision, I navigated those future valleys better:

- With more self-awareness
- With stronger boundaries
- With the mindset that my destiny was mine to control

Field Challenge: Consciously Avoid the Valley (or Climb Out of It)

In your consulting journey:

- Reflect honestly: Are you drifting toward your own Valley of Despair right now?
- If so, make the decision: Will you let consulting define your lifestyle, or will you define it yourself?
- Put the fundamentals into place:

- Protect your body's energy
- Nurture your mind's clarity
- Invest intentionally in your relationships
- Design your week around sustainability, not just productivity

Final Word: The Valley Is Where You Find Your Power

The Valley of Despair isn't something to fear. It's where you earn the wisdom that sustains your career. It's where you prove to yourself that your life and career belong to you, not your calendar or your firm. And when you climb out of that first valley with intention, you'll discover something profound:

- You become a healthier, more resilient, and more balanced consultant.
- Your relationships outside of work thrive because they're treated as priorities, not distractions.
- Your clients get a better version of you, one who is focused, calm, present, and committed.
- Your career flourishes because you're in it for the long game.

You may face valleys again, but they'll never own you. That's the real secret to consulting as a sustainable, fulfilling, impactful career.

12

Consulting as a Craft and Calling

"Consulting isn't just a career path—it can be a way of life. A craft to hone. A calling to fulfill. A legacy to leave."

A Higher Standard

After everything we've discussed, mindset, process, frame-works, trust, execution, value, relationships, and well-being, it all points to this fundamental question:

- How will you show up as a consultant?
- What will your work stand for?
- What kind of legacy will you leave behind when the client, team, or project is long over?

Consulting can easily become a transactional grind if you let it.

Or... it can be something more: A craft to master, a calling to answer. The Difference Between a Job, a Career, and a Craft

A job is something you do for income. A career is a path you follow for achievement and advancement. A craft is something you intentionally refine over time, a lifelong pursuit of excellence and purpose. When you embrace consulting as your calling, you unlock deeper meaning. You stop asking, "What's the next project or promotion?" You start asking, "How can I truly serve?"

Craftsmanship: The Quiet Edge

Craft is about depth, care, attention to detail, discipline, and continual improvement.

In consulting, craftsmanship shows up when you:

- · Ask better, deeper, bolder questions
- · Improve your frameworks with every engagement
- · Sharpen your ability to synthesize complex information into clarity
- · Deliver quality without shortcuts
- · Take pride in the small moments of excellence that no one else may notice, but you know matter

Craftsmanship gives you an edge that no AI or playbook can replicate. It's what transforms consulting from a job into a lifelong skillset that compounds over decades.

Calling: Why Purpose Matters

Consulting is hard work. It tests your resilience, intellect, and emotional agility. If your sole motivator is achievement or income, you'll hit a wall eventually, burnout, cynicism, and stagnation.

But if you approach consulting as a calling, your motivation shifts:

- You're driven by impact, not just activity.
- You care deeply about the people you serve—clients, colleagues, teams.
- You become committed to helping others think better, act faster, and succeed sustainably.

Purpose adds staying power. It fuels your energy and keeps you resilient when the pressure rises.

Craft + Calling = Legacy

The consultant who masters their craft and embraces their calling doesn't just deliver projects. They build a legacy.

Your legacy is:

- The leaders you've influenced
- The teams you've developed
- The organizations you've helped transform
- The culture you've improved
- The trust you've earned

At the end of your consulting journey, these are the things that matter, not the number of billable hours or project milestones completed.

The Human Side of Consulting Will Always Endure

In this AI-first era, knowledge and analysis are increasingly automated. Templates are everywhere. Slide decks can be generated in minutes.

But what will never be commoditized is:

- Your judgment
- Your ability to sense what matters most in a room
- Your capacity for empathy and listening
- Your courage to challenge a client when it's hard
- Your steadiness under pressure
- Your presence as a trusted partner

These human qualities will define the consultants who thrive for decades to come.

Living the Calling: The Consultant's Inner Compass

When consulting becomes your craft and calling, you stop measuring success by conventional metrics.

You begin to ask yourself:

- Did I help my client see clearly today?
- Did I simplify complexity?
- Did I serve the real need, not just the stated ask?
- Did I make this team better than I found it?
- Did I honor my values and protect my health, mind, and relationships along the way?

That's mastery.

The Privilege and Responsibility of Consulting

Consulting is a profession of profound privilege:

- You get invited into complex, high-stakes challenges.
- You help leaders navigate decisions that shape businesses and lives.
- You influence strategies that impact entire industries.

But with that privilege comes responsibility:

- To do the work with care and quality
- To treat your clients' businesses as if they were your own
- To respect people as well as problems
- To balance confidence with humility
- To leave a positive mark on every team and organization you touch

Field Challenge: Define Your Craft + Calling

Take time this week to reflect intentionally:

- What part of your work do you want to master, not just complete?
- How will you design a consulting life that sustains you, body, mind, and relationships?
- Where does your consulting work intersect with your personal sense of purpose?
- How will you ensure that every project is a platform for craftsmanship and meaning?

Final Word: The Modern Consultant's Path

The consulting profession is changing faster than ever, but the fundamentals endure. Clients won't remember how polished your slide deck was. They'll remember how you made them feel during difficult decisions. They'll remember the clarity you brought when things felt chaotic. They'll remember that you cared enough to do the work well and to make them better along the way. That's what it means to treat consulting as a craft and a calling.

When you live this way:

- You protect your energy and health
- You honor your relationships
- You deliver transformative outcomes
- You elevate every client, colleague, and project you touch

And that's when consulting stops being work and starts being your way of contributing to something larger.

That's mastery.

That's meaning.

That's the modern consultant's higher path.

Epilogue

The Consultant of the Future

"The future belongs to those who adapt—but stay anchored in what matters most."

As you close this book, remember this:

- The world around us is transforming faster than ever.
- AI isn't coming, it's already here.
- It's changing how people work, how organizations operate, and how value is created.

And while these tools will accelerate everything, they won't replace what makes a great consultant indispensable. The future will demand that you adapt your methods, tools, and processes with speed and agility, but it will also demand that you hold tightly to the timeless qualities that define world-class consulting:

- Empathy
- Judgment
- Courage

- Clarity
- Trust
- Integrity

These are your differentiators.

What's Next? You've now seen the mindset, process, and practices of the modern consultant laid out in these pages.

The challenge is this:

- Don't just think differently, act differently.
- Treat consulting as a craft, a discipline to hone every day.
- Embrace it as a calling, a meaningful way to serve clients and organizations in times of unprecedented complexity.

And above all:

- Use AI and technology to amplify your impact, but stay human in how you lead, communicate, and connect.

A Final Thought

The consultants who will thrive in the future won't be the ones who simply work harder, memorize frameworks, or chase tools.

They'll be the ones who:

- Adapt with curiosity and humility

- Think deeply but act decisively
- Show up with care for clients and teams
- Stay relentlessly focused on delivering value
- Invest in themselves, not just professionally, but personally: protecting their body, mind, and relationships so they can sustain excellence over the long haul

This is your opportunity.

You have everything you need to lead, not just participate in this next era of consulting.

Go forward.
Be bold.
Stay grounded.
Serve well.

Be the consultant the future will remember.

Notes

FRAMEWORKS THAT WORK

1   Barbara Minto, *The Pyramid Principle: Logic in Writing and Thinking*, 3rd ed. (Financial Times Prentice Hall, 2009).

2   Michael E. Porter, *Competitive Advantage*: Creating and Sustaining Superior Performance (The Free Press, 1985).

3   Andrew Campbell, Mark Margetts, and Sven Kunisch, *Operating Model Canvas: Aligning Operations and Organization with Strategy* (Van Haren Publishing, 2017).

BECOMING A TRUSTED ADVISOR

4   David H. Maister, Charles H. Green, and Robert M. Galford, *The Trusted Advisor* (Free Press, 2000).